Discovering Norway

A Comprehensive Travel Guide to the Land of Fjords and Northern Lights

By

Joanne Vanhorn

All rights reserved. No part of this publication may be reproduced, distributed, or transmitted in any form or by any means, including photocopying, recording, or other electronic or mechanical methods, without the prior written permission of the publisher, except in the case of brief quotations embodied in critical reviews and certain other noncommercial uses permitted by copyright law.

Copyright©(Joanne,Vanhorn), (2023).

Table of Contents:

Chapter 1

A Snippet of Norwegian History

Chapter 2

Norway travel guide

Chapter 3

Expectations for a Trip to Norway.

Chapter 4

Malls in Norway

Chapter 5

Travel Advice for Norway

Chapter 1

A Snippet of Norwegian History

The Sami people, who have lived in Norway's northern areas for thousands of years, are the country's first inhabitants. Around the eighth century, during the Viking Age, Norwegian seamen built trade networks and towns all across Europe and beyond, developing a reputation as expert navigators and warriors. Following the introduction of Christianity in the 11th century, Norway evolved into a feudal nation with a powerful central monarchy.

After joining Denmark in the Kalmar Union at the end of the 14th century, Norway was ruled by Denmark for the following four centuries. Norway saw substantial economic and social upheaval throughout this time, including the emergence of a merchant elite and the expansion of industry in the 19th century.

Norway separated from Denmark in 1905, establishing a constitutional monarchy headed by King Haakon VII. Norway was occupied by Nazi Germany during World War II, but following the war, the nation went through a period of fast economic growth and social advancement, in part due to its enormous natural resources, such as oil and gas.

Norway, a wealthy and developed nation today, is renowned for its high quality of living, forward-thinking social policies, and dedication to environmental sustainability. With a population of over 5 million, the majority of whom are of Norwegian heritage, it also has sizable Sami, immigrant, and refugee populations.

Chapter 2

Norway travel guide

Norway is a lovely and varied nation with a lot to offer tourists, including breathtaking natural landscapes and a rich cultural legacy. An itinerary for your vacation to Norway is provided below:

Norway is a year-round vacation location, but the ideal time to go will depend on your interests.

While the winter months (December–February) provide chances for skiing, snowboarding, and watching the Northern Lights, the summer months (June–August) are best for outdoor activities like hiking and kayaking.

Stunning fjords like the well-known Geirangerfjord and Naeroyfjord, which may be explored by boat or kayak, are among Norway's must-see attractions. The lively metropolis of Bergen, the ancient city of Trondheim, and the scenic town of Flam are a few other must-see locations. The Hardangervidda, Rondane, and Jotunheimen national parks are all recommended for nature enthusiasts to explore.

Outdoor activities: Activities like hiking, skiing, kayaking, fishing, and cycling are all readily available in Norway. Additionally, the nation is a well-liked location for dog sledding, whale watching, and witnessing the Northern Lights.

Food and drink: Locally produced foods like reindeer, berries, and shellfish are the foundation of Norwegian cuisine. Fish soup, smoked salmon, and reindeer stew are among the meals you must try. In addition, Norway is renowned for its traditional Scandinavian spirit, aquavit, as well as its artisan breweries.

Norway boasts a sophisticated public transportation network that includes buses, trains, and ferries. The gorgeous roadways of the nation can also be explored by renting a car.

Norway has a variety of lodging alternatives, from high-end hotels to inexpensive hostels. Another well-liked choice is camping, and there are many sites available in beautiful settings.

Culture and history: There are several museums, art galleries, and historical places to visit in Norway, which has a rich cultural past. Highlights include the ancient Bryggen Wharf in Bergen, the Bergen Art Museum, and the Viking Ship Museum in Oslo.

Practical advice: Because of Norway's high cost of living, it's crucial to budget well. Additionally, there are stringent alcohol laws in the nation, with restrictions on when beer and wine may be bought. Finally, keep in mind to prepare appropriately because Norway, especially in the summer, can be rather chilly and wet.

Norway is a distinct and intriguing travel location that has something to offer everyone. Norway is certain to make an impact, whether you're seeking outdoor adventure, culture, and history, or simply taking in the breathtaking natural beauty.

Chapter 3

Expectations for a Trip to Norway.

There are several things you might anticipate if you're thinking about visiting Norway.

Beautiful natural scenery: From magnificent fjords and towering mountains to sparkling lakes and lush forests, Norway is recognized for its gorgeous natural settings. You may anticipate continuously being surrounded by amazing natural beauty whether you're hiking, skiing, or just driving through the countryside.

Cold climate: Norway is a northern nation, thus the winters may be quite cold there. To be warm and comfortable throughout your visit, bring warm clothing such as a quality jacket, hat, and gloves.

High costs: Norway is renowned for having a high cost of living, which also affects the travel and tourism sector. You should budget more money than you may in other nations for meals, lodging, and activities.

Despite their high costs, Norwegians are renowned for being hospitable and kind. Everywhere you go, you can count on being welcomed with a smile and some useful information.

The public transportation system in Norway is quite effective and includes buses, trains, and ferries. Even in more isolated locations, traveling the nation will be simple and effective.

Outdoor pursuits: With a wealth of chances for hiking, skiing, fishing, and other outdoor pursuits, Norway is a sanctuary for outdoor lovers. Norway offers a wide variety of outdoor activities for those who like being in the great outdoors.

One-of-a-kind cultural experiences: Norway has a rich cultural legacy, and there are many opportunities to have memorable experiences, such as seeing historic stave churches and Viking museums and trying local cuisines like lutefisk and rakfisk.

Overall, visiting Norway may be an immensely rewarding experience if you're ready for the harsh climate and expensive accommodations. Norway is a destination that should be on your vacation wish list because of its breathtaking natural beauty, friendly population, and wealth of outdoor activities.

"Must-see sights" while visiting Norway

Norway is a stunning nation with stunning natural landscapes and deep cultural history. Its varied scenery includes craggy mountains, breathtaking fjords, quaint villages, and thriving cities.

The following sights are a must-see when visiting Norway:

Geirangerfjord: The Geirangerfjord, which lies in western Norway, is a UNESCO World Heritage Site renowned for its breathtaking beauty. It is a well-liked location for cruises and sightseeing because of the towering mountains, gushing waterfalls, and crystal-clear blue seas that surround it.

Bergen is the second-largest city in Norway and a center for cultural and creative endeavors. It is well-known for its vibrant wooden buildings, lovely waterfront, and historical locations like the Hanseatic Museum and Bryggen Wharf.

One of the greatest spots to observe the Northern Lights, also known as the Aurora Borealis, is Norway. In the northern regions of Norway, like Troms, between September and April is the ideal time to observe them.

Oslo: Oslo, the capital of Norway, is a thriving, international metropolis with a significant cultural and historical past. The Munch Museum and the Viking Ship Museum are just a few of the galleries and museums that call it home.

National Park of Jotunheimen:

Centrally located in Norway, the hilly Jotunheimen National Park is a well-liked place to go skiing and hiking. The tallest mountain in Norway, Galdhopiggen, is one of its many peaks.

Trolltunga: Situated in southwest Norway, Trolltunga is a magnificent rock structure. It is a well-liked trekking location and provides breathtaking views of the surroundings.

The biggest and deepest fjord in Norway is called Sognefjord, and it extends more than 200 kilometers inland. It is renowned for its breathtaking landscape, which includes mountains, waterfalls, and glaciers.

Lofoten Islands: Off Norway's northern coast, there lies a collection of islands known as the Lofoten Islands. They are well-known for their striking scenery, charming fishing towns, and chances for hiking, fishing, and wildlife viewing.

Preikestolen is a flat-topped cliff in southwest Norway that is often referred to as the Pulpit Rock. It is a well-liked hiking spot and provides breathtaking views of the Lysefjord below.

Flm Railway: You may enjoy a beautiful train trip through the breathtaking Norwegian landscape on the Flam Railway. The surrounding mountains and fjords may be seen in spectacular detail from one of the steepest railway lines in the world.

These are just a handful of Norway's must-see sights. Norway is a place that everyone should visit due to its breathtaking natural beauty and rich cultural history.

Chapter 4

Malls in Norway.

When visiting Norway, tourists should be prepared to find shopping malls.

In different cities around Norway, several shopping centers provide a wide range of retail experiences. When visiting Norway, tourists may anticipate finding a variety of services and entertainment alternatives, as well as contemporary, well-designed retail complexes featuring a mix of national and worldwide brands. When visiting shopping centers in Norway, keep in mind the following:

Wide selection of businesses: The majority of Norway's shopping centers include a variety of shops, including clothing stores, electronics stores, bookstores, beauty salons, and more. Both well-known worldwide and distinctively Norwegian local brands are available.

Shopping malls in Norway contain a variety of cafés and restaurants that serve both local and foreign food. There are sit-down restaurants, quick food restaurants, and coffee shops that can accommodate a variety of preferences and price ranges.

Entertainment options: In Norway, there are several shopping malls with movie theaters, bowling lanes, and gaming arcades. These provide for enjoyable times spent with loved ones, particularly on gloomy or chilly days.

Shopping centers in Norway also include a variety of convenience services, including pharmacies, supermarkets, and ATMs. Because of this, taking care of necessities while shopping is simple.

Design and architecture: The architecture and design of Norway's shopping malls reflect the country's reputation for contemporary and minimalist style. Expect to see modern, elegant structures with plenty of windows and open areas.

Overall, Norway's shopping centers provide a contemporary and practical shopping experience with a variety of domestic and foreign brands, entertainment choices, and convenience services.

They are wonderful locations to spend some time eating, shopping, and taking in the local culture.

When visiting Norway, a visitor should be prepared for "accommodations".

Norway is a lovely nation with a lot to offer, including breathtaking natural scenery and distinctive cultural experiences. Depending on their interests and budget, guests may anticipate a variety of lodging alternatives.

When traveling to Norway, the following kinds of hotels are typical:

Hotels: There are many hotels in Norway, ranging in price from inexpensive to magnificent. In cities and towns, many hotels provide services like free Wi-Fi, breakfast, and in-room amenities like TVs, minibars, and coffee machines.

Norway has a variety of cabins and cottages that are ideal for nature enthusiasts if you want to explore the great outdoors. These are often found in isolated locations and provide basic conveniences like heating, kitchens, and common restrooms along with a homey, warm atmosphere.

Hostels are an excellent choice if you're traveling on a tight budget. They provide dormitory-style lodging with communal amenities including kitchens and baths. For people who want more solitude, several hostels also have private rooms.

Camping: The stunning natural environment of Norway is well-known, and camping is a common method to take it all in. There are many campgrounds around the nation with amenities including showers, toilets, and laundry services, both in the countryside and close to urban areas.

Airbnb: If you want a more individualized experience, this website has a variety of unusual lodging options, including apartments, homes, and cabins. From a nice apartment in the city to a secluded lodge in the highlands, everything is available.

In Norway, you can count on a high standard of cleanliness and comfort regardless of the kind of accommodation you choose. Because of the well-known warmth and friendliness of Norwegians, the majority of lodgings provide top-notch service to make sure your stay is pleasant.

Norway's outdoor activities.

When visiting Norway, tourists can anticipate engaging in outdoor activities.

Norway, with its stunning landscapes, fjords, mountains, and forests, is a haven for outdoor enthusiasts. Here are a few outdoor activities that visitors to Norway may partake in:

Hiking: The world's most picturesque hiking paths may be found in Norway. For those wanting excitement and breathtaking vistas, the well-known Trolltunga and Preikestolen walks are fantastic. The several national parks, including Jotunheimen,

Rondane, and Hardangervidda, are also accessible for exploration.

Skiing and snowboarding: With several ski resorts providing top-notch skiing and snowboarding, Norway is a winter paradise. Some of the greatest snow experiences in the nation may be found at the resorts in Trysil, Hemsedal, or Geilo.

Fishing: Norway is a great place for fishing aficionados since it has a lot of rivers and lakes that are home to salmon and trout. For a chance to catch some of the largest fish in the world, hire a guide or sign up for a fishing excursion.

Kayaking and canoeing: Some of the most beautiful and spectacular kayaking and canoeing experiences may be had in Norway's fjords, lakes, and rivers. For a tranquil experience, kayak through the congested fjords or explore the serene lakes and streams.

Bicycle: The nation of Norway is home to a network of bicycle routes that will take you through some of the most stunning and diverse landscapes. The Rallarvegen is a well-known cycling path that passes through beautiful alpine scenery.

Rock climbing: Norway has some of the world's top rock climbing locations. Consider climbing the Kjerag, a well-known peak in the Lysefjorden, for a difficult climb and breathtaking scenery.

Whale watching: Many whales, including orcas and humpbacks, may be seen along Norway's coastline. To have a chance to view these majestic animals up close, go on a whale-watching excursion.

These are just a handful of the many outdoor activities that visitors to Norway may enjoy.

Norway has something to offer everyone, whether they are looking for adventure, leisure, or breathtaking natural beauty.

Transportation Costs to Norway

When visiting Norway, travelers should budget for their transportation costs.

It's crucial to keep in mind that Norway is recognized for being rather pricey in comparison to other places when it comes to transportation expenditures. Travelers may choose from a variety of modes of transportation, each with a different price tag.

Travelers may utilize the local buses, trams, and metros to move about in major cities including Oslo, Bergen, and Trondheim. The price of a single ticket normally ranges from 30 to 40 NOK (about $3 to USD 4), while the price of a day pass is around 105 NOK (about USD 11). It's important to remember that public transit options outside of big cities may be restricted, so make sure your travel plans take that into account.

Taxis: Taxis are readily accessible in most cities and towns, and their prices are governed by law. The initial price is around 100 NOK (USD 11), with an extra 18–20 NOK (USD 2) for each subsequent kilometer. However, it's crucial to budget appropriately since cabs in Norway may be extremely pricey.

Renting a vehicle is a fantastic choice for tourists who wish to experience Norway's stunning landscape. Expect to spend between 500 and 800 NOK (about $58 and 88 USD) each day, while costs vary based on the kind of vehicle and rental agency. Gas costs should be taken into account since they might be fairly costly in Norway.

Domestic flights are a practical alternative if you're going great distances inside Norway. The cost of a one-way ticket varies based on the airline and the season, but you should budget at least 500 NOK (about USD 55).

Railway: The railway system in Norway is well-developed, and trains provide a convenient and effective means to travel between cities. Prices vary based on the route and season, but one-way tickets typically cost between 300 and 500 NOK (about $33-55 USD).

Budgeting properly is essential since travel expenses in Norway may be rather high. Travelers may choose from a variety of transportation alternatives, each of which has advantages and disadvantages.

Norwegian Cuisine and Drinks

When visiting Norway, tourists may anticipate certain foods and beverages.

Seafood, wild game, and dairy products are heavily emphasized in Norwegian cuisine, which is distinguished by its concentration on locally and freshly procured foods. Visitors visiting Norway may anticipate finding a range of unusual and delectable dishes and beverages. Here are a few of the most well-known:

Salmon, cod, and herring are among the premium seafood options available in Norway. These fish may be enjoyed by visitors in several ways, such as smoked, grilled, and cured. The typical Norwegian delicacies lutefisk (lye-soaked dried fish), rakfisk (fermented fish), and skrei (cod) can also be of interest to seafood enthusiasts.

Game foods: Hunting is a well-liked activity in Norway, where a variety of game meats, such as reindeer, moose, and venison, are produced. Visitors may sample these meats in recipes like venison burgers and reindeer stew.

Products of the dairy industry: Norway is renowned for its premium cheese, butter, and cream. Brown cheese (brunost), a cheese that is only found in Norway, is created from caramelized goat's milk and tastes nutty and sweet.

Knekkebrod: A variety of grains, seeds, and nuts are used to make this kind of crispbread in Norway. It's a common snack that often includes cheese, meats, and spreads.

Traditional Norwegian liqueur known as aquavit is prepared from potatoes or grains and flavored with dill or caraway. It is often offered as a digestif after a meal.

Beer: Visitors to Norway may sample a range of locally made beers thanks to the country's booming craft beer culture. Pilsners, stouts, and farmhouse ales are a few popular beer varieties in Norway.

Coffee: With a thriving coffee culture, Norway is one of the world's top users of the beverage. Traditional black coffee (svart kaffe), cappuccinos, and lattes are among the selection of coffee beverages available to visitors.

Overall, tourists visiting Norway may anticipate discovering a wide range of distinctive and delectable dishes and beverages that emphasize the nation's regional ingredients and culinary traditions.

When to Visit Norway

The ideal season to go to Norway

Norway is a fascinating nation that draws tourists from all over the globe to see its breathtaking landscapes, natural treasures, and distinctive culture. The activities and sights you choose to see during your vacation will determine the ideal time to visit Norway.

Norway is most often visited during the summer (June to August), particularly for outdoor pursuits like hiking, bicycling, fishing, and sightseeing. The nation has temperate weather, lengthy days, and even up to 24 hours of daylight in certain regions. You may go on a cruise, take a fjord tour, or attend outdoor festivals and activities.

The greatest time to go to Norway if you like winter activities like skiing, snowboarding, and dog sledding is from December through February. You may enjoy the Northern Lights, which are visible in many areas of the nation, and the stunning snow-covered landscapes. Be ready, however, for shorter days and chillier weather.

The shoulder seasons of spring (March-May) and fall (September-November) might be wonderful times to visit Norway if you want to escape the crowds and enjoy warmer weather. These are beautiful times of year to visit because of the spring and autumn wildflower blooms, respectively.

During this season, it's a good idea to prepare for a variety of weather situations since Norway's weather may be unexpected. Furthermore, Norway is a well-liked tourist destination, so to prevent disappointment, it's important to reserve your lodging and activities much in advance.

Chapter 5

Travel Advice for Norway

Here are some helpful pointers and recommendations for a visitor to Norway:

Dress accordingly. Even in the height of summer, Norway can be rather chilly, so be sure to carry layers of warm clothes, a waterproof jacket, and sturdy walking shoes.

You can expect to spend hefty expenses for food, lodging, and transportation as Norway is one of the most expensive places in the world.

Make use of the great public transportation system in Norway, which includes buses, trains, and ferries. This may help you travel more cheaply around the nation.

Check the weather forecast before you leave the house since Norway may encounter all kinds of weather. You may use this to arrange your activities appropriately.

Try the local cuisine: Unique and delectable foods like salmon, reindeer, and brown cheese can be found in Norway. Don't be hesitant to give anything new a try!

Due to Norway's famous natural beauty, it is crucial to protect the environment and leave no mark while going on outdoor adventures.

Even though most people in Norway speak English, it's always appreciated when visitors make an effort to learn a few Norwegian words.

Benefit from the long daylight hours:
Since Norway has long daylight hours in the summer, you may pack in more activities and go exploring for longer.

Know the proper time to go if you want to view the Northern Lights:
If you want to see the Northern Lights, you should go from late September to early April, and you should choose a location with a clear sky and little light pollution.

Plan: To prevent disappointment, it's crucial to schedule lodgings and activities well in advance while visiting Norway, particularly during the busiest time of year.

With these hints and recommendations, I hope you have a wonderful vacation in Norway!

Travel Safety Measures for Norway

What safety precautions and regulations should visitors to Norway be aware of.

Norway is renowned for its breathtaking scenery, extensive cultural legacy, and secure atmosphere. To guarantee a safe and pleasurable journey, it's important to be informed of the safety measures and regulations that are in place in Norway. The following are some safety guidelines and regulations that visitors to Norway should be aware of:

COVID-19 safety measures: As of May 2023, the COVID-19 pandemic is still active, and Norway has taken several steps to safeguard its citizens and tourists. Travelers should be ready to adhere to any COVID-19 safety regulations that may be in effect during their trip, such as face mask use in indoor public areas, social withdrawal, and presenting documentation of immunization or a negative test result.

Driving safety: If you want to drive or hire a vehicle in Norway, be aware that road conditions may be difficult owing to the nation's mountainous geography and unpredictable weather. Always buckle up, follow all traffic laws and signage, and steer clear of driving when intoxicated or high.

Outdoor safety: Although visitors are drawn to Norway's natural beauty, it's crucial to be aware of any risks when hiking, skiing, or engaging in other outdoor sports. Before setting out, always check the weather forecast and trail conditions, pack the necessary supplies, and notify someone of your plan and anticipated return time.

Wildlife protection: A wide range of animals, such as moose, reindeer, wolves, and bears, may be found in Norway. Keep a safe distance from any wildlife you come across, don't feed it, and abide by any rules or regulations that may be in effect.

Swimming, boating, and fishing are all popular water sports that may be enjoyed in Norway's various fjords, lakes, and rivers. However, currents and meteorological conditions may vary fast, and water temperatures can be frigid all year long. Always swim in specified places, use a life jacket, and be aware of any safety regulations or limits that could be in effect.

Norway is seen to be a secure nation with few crimes, but travelers should still take security measures to keep themselves and their things safe. Avoid going alone in strange places after dark, keep your valuables in a secure location, and pay attention to your surroundings.

Visitors may have a safe and enjoyable journey to Norway by adhering to these safety regulations and procedures.

Printed in Great Britain
by Amazon